MASTER YOUR LIFE

MASTER YOUR LIFE

EARN THE ULTIMATE DEGREE IN YOU AND LIVE WITH PURPOSE, HAPPINESS, AND DISCOVERY

CHRISTI BURTON

BEYOND
BELIEF
—PUBLISHING—
YOU HOLD THE FUTURE IN YOUR HANDS

*A digital copy of Ph.ME! Plan referenced in this book is free with the purchase of this book. Visit phmeplan.com and send code: PHDMASTERYOURLIFE to the contact email.

ISBN: 978-1-957972-09-1

To my dad, who knows how to make a grown adult daughter feel like his little girl—swooping in at the right time to make things okay again. And, to my mom in heaven, whose creative spirit is what I draw upon daily.

PRAISE FOR
MASTER YOUR LIFE

"Prioritize YOU: A blueprint for fulfillment. This book is a compass for anyone feeling overwhelmed, helping them chart a course toward personal fulfillment. The combination of insightful wisdom and actionable steps encourages readers to embrace self-discovery, cultivate meaningful connections, and embark on a journey that integrates passion, purpose, and a deep appreciation for the beauty of life."

— Dame Marie Diamond
Feng Shui and Law of Attraction Master
www.mariediamond.com

"Dive into the transformative journey of *Master Your Life* and unlock the power within you to create an abundant and fulfilled life. Embrace the belief that a bright and beautiful future is not only possible, it is also within your grasp. Claim it now."

— Michael Bernard Beckwith
Founder & CEO, Agape International Spiritual Center
Author, *Life Visioning and Spiritual Liberation*
Host of *Take Back Your Mind* Podcast

"Create a life of clarity, purpose, growth, connections, and adventure! *Master Your Life* will give you the jumpstart you need to live a better life… one that you are excited is actually YOURS!"

— Joe Vitale
Featured Teacher in the Hit Movie, *The Secret*
Author of *The Attractor Factor*

Contents

Acknowledgments

I was inspired to write this book by several people and by some of my own life aspirations. One individual, also known as *my favorite human*, is my niece, Sidney, who humored me by participating in my idea for Pandemic To-Do Lists in the spring of 2020. Those lists ultimately sparked the idea for a product I decided to call Ph.ME! Plan, which are *Get*-To-Do Lists rather than the traditional, and often dreaded, To-Do Lists. But because of this idea, my talented little sidekick dabbled in art—an item she had put on her list—and realized she was actually quite good.

Another inspiration was *my sweet Marti*. My mom passed away when I was twenty-three, but God blessed me with another chance at having a mom figure, and she was Marti. She is the woman I will forever think of when someone asks a question, and you reply by saying that you don't know the answer.

As Marti always said, "Well, dahlin', do you want to know, or do you want to wonder?"

I want to know. I also want to be able to say *dahlin'* with as much charm as my sweet Marti, but for now I'll be happy hitting up Google to find answers.

Foreword

It is an inspiring opportunity to be able to introduce you to Christi Burton's new book, *Master Your Life: Earn the Ultimate Degree in YOU and Live with Purpose, Happiness, and Discovery.* As an advocate for many years of human transformation and aligning our primary objectives to our higher values, I found her insights into maximizing growth, development, and actions that lead to a life of adventure, human connection, and meaning to be authentic, relatable, and truly inspiring.

In this book, Christi shares impactful personal stories, compelling research, and heartfelt wisdom on how to live a life of purpose and fulfillment. She offers practical advice on how to set achievable goals, overcome obstacles, and create a life that is truly worth living. A refreshing sense of humor throughout makes this read delightful.

Whether you are seeking to improve your career, your relationships, or your well-being, *Master Your Life: Earn the Ultimate Degree in YOU and Live with Purpose, Happiness, and Discovery* is the perfect guide to help you make your dreams a reality. I highly recommend this book, and the coordinating product, the Ph.ME! Plan, to anyone seeking to take their life to the next level.

~Dr. John Demartini
Human Behavior Expert
Polymath
Internationally Published Author

Introduction

My thing has always been organizing. I'm like Monica on the TV show *Friends*, and a junk drawer's worst nightmare. I have organized friends' and family members' closets, pantries, and offices, and I secretly love it. Organizers like me enjoy keeping tangible objects in place; that, in turn, keeps our mental state intact.

This attribute of mine is also what led to creating Ph.ME! Plan and writing this book. The name for the product came from my desire to have the highest level of knowledge of what it takes to be the ruler of my own life. I wanted a Ph.ME! degree in Christi Burton.

I wanted to understand and live out my purpose—to live a life filled with joy and to experience authentic, heart-pounding, mouth-dropping adventure. I wanted to know my very existence has meant something worthwhile to others. To do all these things meant establishing personal goals, big and small, and making a point of following through without putting them aside for the To-Do List items in life.

I by no means am an expert on a healthy, balanced life. In fact, I am one who NEEDS more balance and craves more time with my friends and family and me-time. But like many others, I allow myself to get caught up in tasks WAY too often and lose sight of what's really important. And that is … living life! I hope this book and the Ph.ME! Plan motivate you to chase your dreams—I mean seriously chase them down!— learn new skills, connect with others, and start making dreams and goals an even bigger priority than picking up your laundry. I hope you are inspired and begin pursuing a PhD in *your* life.

Let's turn those goals into realities! It is as easy as writing things down.

Goals that are not written down are just wishes.

~ unknown

Are you the master of your life?

The best way to genuinely answer that is by looking back at each week and asking yourself these questions:

- *Did I have an incredible week, or did I just go through a week that highly resembles the one before it and the one before that?*

- *Did I center my activities around doing for others—my employer or perhaps my family?*

- *Did I get so wrapped up in work and my To-Do lists that I became too tired or too frazzled to fit in the activities I generally love doing?*

- *Did I live in a manner I wish to continue, or one that leaves me wanting to learn more from exposure to something new, connecting more with those I love being around, and experiencing more fun, excitement, and purpose?*

- *Did I incorporate new hobbies, find time to pursue entrepreneurial ventures, or engage in activities that made me feel like a kid again?*

If your answers repeatedly point to a life you do not wish to settle for, what is stopping you from living a thrilling life? I can tell you what stops me, and in the same breath, I will tell you it is the main reason I have written this book.

What has stopped me? The comfort of doing the same things over and over. Becoming so good at it that it feels like a win each week to get things done better or perhaps quicker than I did the previous week. Seeing improvement in even mundane activities does provide a sense of accomplishment. While it feels like a small step in the right direction, I can honestly say many of those qualities are not what I'd want to hang my hat on. Some are, but I often do not prioritize living a happy life over my Must-Do tasks each week.

Friends, I have lived that *running on a hamster wheel* life too. Do I want to live this way forever, doing for others my whole life? Not really. I want to do a great job in my career because I truly love what I do, and I feel very blessed to be where I am. But I also want to feel that way when I'm off the clock.

I started this book for me—as a reminder of what is needed to live a life of joy rather than one I stroll through each day with nothing new to answer when someone asks, "How was your day?" I finished this book knowing I wrote it for millions of others as well; I am not alone. I want everyone who reads this to live the life they dream of too.

And yes, I am the person who constantly speaks positively—sunshine and rainbows, even in the face of storm clouds. It's because I believe every bit of what I am saying is valid. If a dream is in your heart, it's because God put it there. Don't let it go to waste and continue putting it off by being sedentary in your own life. Big or small—chase that sucker down.

I recently heard a Joel Osteen sermon that said something I will never forget. He said if your desire is not coming true, but you're not going after it with all you've got, then, respectfully, you just don't want it badly enough. Do you feel like that could be you? I sometimes do. Joel's voice pops into my head with that phrase whenever I think of something I'd like to do, but I'm not doing it. And it is like a kick in the pants to get up and move toward what I want.

So, congratulations for going on this journey of pursuing excitement, happiness, and purpose in your own life and seeking an existence in which you will undoubtedly be able to say that there was nothing left you wanted to learn, express, or experience. By the end of this book, you will have an abundance of tools, stories, data, statistics, and tips to help you accomplish any goal in life. And you will probably have created lots of new goals by the time you finish.

My wish for you is this: By regularly using your Ph.ME! Plan—a free download with the purchase of this book—in combination with the tools and information gained from *Master Your Life*, you will become the ultimate authority of *you*. And that, my friend, is the most important thing we can achieve in today's world. I also think you will have a lot of fun going through this process.

Enjoy the journey, adventures, excitement, friendships, emotions, success, well-being, discovery, enlightenment, and happiness that are about to come your way.

How It Began

The concept of the Ph.ME! Plan came to me when the worldwide pandemic began. I was stuck at home like everyone else. To avoid boredom and, quite honestly, loneliness, I sought refuge with my family. I was working from home and was getting up early every day to continue as regular a routine as possible.

Then came the layoffs. I have to say I wasn't surprised because I worked in the wholesale gift industry, and any type of shopping was about as common as toilet paper at the time. And for the first moment in my lifetime, everyone around the globe shared one thing—an uncertainty of what the future held coupled with enough worry to fill a football stadium. The unimaginable had happened. Our world was at a standstill, and billions were waiting for normalcy to resume.

But not I. That mainly is because I am not one to sit still well, as those who know me best are well aware. My idea of sitting still typically requires a notepad, my laptop, and snacks. I'm also a list person. Lists are my primary way of staying organized. During the quarantine, I started writing on my note-taking app every day, which included career-related projects that I wanted to remain focused on. Without a job, I knew that reinventing myself might be crucial to stand out when applying for new employment when competition would surely reach its peak.

Energized by collaboration, I naturally included my family in this little initiative. I gave them a note with instructions to write down what they'd like to accomplish. Can you imagine the list of a teenage girl with no school? Yeah, that was a challenge, but, as always, she was a good sport in humoring her aunt.

As the world slowed down and we had more time on our hands, the concept of writing down what we wanted to accomplish changed a little bit. Hobbies and other skills I had always wanted to learn made their way to my weekly list. During this strange time, I realized there would never be another point in my life where I would have so much available time to devote to learning fun, new things. And, truth be told, I was excited about having free time for once, with fewer responsibilities and more time to research and start pursuits I enjoyed.

Although having more time to dabble in new interests was great, the thought of having no job was as comfortable as camping in the woods with no tent and freezing temperatures. So I decided to hop online and find which skills were listed for all the jobs I was looking for. I started writing what I wanted to learn and sought online courses and resources. I was making daily and weekly task lists to stay on track. I was on a mission. Doing all this filled me with a sense of purpose every day. I also gained hope that, by the end of the chaos, I would wind up even better than before.

Throughout this period, it seemed that, for many people, their inner child surfaced as they immersed themselves in new hobbies. The pandemic also allowed many of us to meet people we may not have otherwise. As someone who has always been interested in learning more and broadening my talents, I relished adding new activities to my list. One, in particular, was writing.

Shortly after identifying my love of writing, I connected with my friend Jenn, who did occasional writing projects for a London-based PR agency. I began walking with her regularly—so much so the tread on my running shoes quickly began to tell the story of my daily journeys. The walks included strategy sessions on how we planned to achieve specific goals. I felt healthier and became empowered and motivated to achieve the life I'd always wanted but had never taken the time to plan and then live out.

During my time with Jenn, who is seriously like the human form of Google, I realized it was not that difficult to start copywriting professionally. She was able to train me quickly on the specifics and pointed me in the direction of online resources. With my degree in communications and background in marketing and sales, it came naturally for me to research and then put my thoughts into a creative brief that others would want to read.

I took free courses and watched several YouTube videos to learn more about copywriting and the industry. It didn't take long for me to become one of the PR agency's leading writers. By connecting with them and writing about hundreds of people reinventing themselves as coaches, mentors, and authors, I realized I didn't have to stop at writing about them and their accomplishments. I could be writing something about myself and celebrating my achievements. And so, *Master Your Life* came to me as a guide for helping others find purpose and create a life they *love* through the Ph.ME! plan, the ultimate of Get-To-Do Lists.

Many people make To-Do Lists but never have I seen one with tasks that enrich our lives. Not until now. Each chapter in this book is devoted to topics that correspond with the plan. With brief explanations, stories, and scientific data about writing down your goals, you can see why each item is so meaningful and a game-changer in life.

I hope everyone who takes advantage of reading this book embraces the Ph.ME! plan and learns to cherish their lives and regain their sense of excitement—the kind kids have on Christmas morning, the kind where you can't wait to jump out of bed every day to have the opportunity to live your extraordinary life.

Even though we all go through uncertain times or occasionally need to reevaluate whether we're living the best way we can, we can still learn, connect with others, and experience activities that add to our sense of balance and peace in life. We can still give back to others to make the world better. Most importantly, we can still make time for adventure and incorporate the highest level of passion for the most precious gift we'll ever have—our own life.

As cheesy as it sounds, don't you want to see that the person staring back at you in the mirror is happy and fulfilled and believes they are living this life on fire? Do you want to see a person with no regrets and no "what ifs"? I want that.

So, what do you say? Let's go on this journey together and earn the highest degree in our own lives—a Ph.ME!

Chapter One

HOW CAN YOU LEARN TO MASTER YOUR LIFE?

Live life with a fire that is never extinguished.
~ unknown

As in any topic one is trying to become an expert, it is necessary to first understand the topic and learn the intricate details. To master your life it is crucial to understand what you want it to encompass and how you want to feel and identify what you want it to represent. The Ph.ME! Plan's intent is to help you create that life you are trying to master.

To learn to master your life, let's start by taking a deeper look at what it is all about. Is your daily or weekly life exciting, rewarding, fulfilling, providing growth opportunities, and fostering a connection with family and friends?

If the answer to that question isn't an enthusiastic yes, then keep reading to learn how the Ph.ME! Plan can help you live a life of purpose and happiness.

- Are you pursuing your dreams and goals, and are they coming to fruition?

- Are you experiencing some joy or adventure regularly, or would you have to stop and think about it if someone asked you when the last time you felt that way was?

- Are you doing one thing a week that lights up your smile like the kind of high you get when you win on a scratch-off ticket?

- Are you excited about your future?

- Do you feel you are on precisely the right track and proud of all you have accomplished and all you will achieve?

- Are you regularly making time for activities that keep you healthy in all regards? Most importantly, do you have the kind of life that is so magical you feel lucky it is yours?

Not many people can truthfully answer yes to the majority of these questions. Not in the way they should, given that each person only gets one go-round. I include myself in this, and that is why I created this book and the accompanying Ph.ME! Plan. I decided to have a life that I am the master of—I want a PhD in ME!

The Ph.ME! Plan is the perfect way to bring all you want in your life to the forefront and help you make and keep them a priority. Ph.ME! Plan will guide you to create and pursue a life you are overjoyed to live, rather than merely exist. Think of them as To-Do Lists of the tasks and activities you want to do.

The purpose of the Ph.ME! Plan and this book is to center, organize, and motivate you daily to bring joy and fulfillment to all areas of your life. And, no, the moments that provide joy do not include *1) pick up dry cleaning, 2) pay water bill, or 3) register child for soccer.* Those written reminders are meant for a sticky note or a shared calendar.

The Ph.ME! Plan includes cards with prompts you fill out weekly to ensure you are living your life with purpose, and they are meant to capture your written notes about health in daily living—physically, spiritually, and mentally—to provide tools to reach your goals and encourage new experiences that keep life thrilling, fun, and filled with connectedness and joy.

Master Your Life provides real-life stories about each category on the plan and illustrates why they are so powerful. It also includes tips for making the most out of your Ph.ME! Plan, examples of varying responses each category can have, and the science behind writing down your dreams and goals.

Dear Self,

I am grateful for my health and comfort in life as I'm seeing many friends and acquaintances having to endure really difficult situations.

I am excited about my upcoming vacation with my boyfriend and our friends and exploring a city we've never been to!

I am happy that God closed doors to job opportunities that were not the right fit for me and what I'm looking for.

I will appreciate and enjoy the journey and not just when I obtain my goals' type of mentality.

one word   Flourish

dreams + goals
1) Buy my dream home!
2) Enjoy a fulfilling/rewarding new career.

projects Create some type of artwork to frame grandparents' old Broadway Playbills.

next steps 1) Research online for inspiration
2) Purchase materials
3) Create an outline

highlight Visit Dad

adventure Schedule long weekend in Asheville with my friends.

self-care   Walk, go to gym, read daily affirmations, face and hair mask.

affirmation/mantra LIVE life – don't just exist!

learn 1) Take master class in writing
2) Take online graphic design course

new skill/hobby   hand lettering

giving Ask God to put someone in my life that I can be a blessing to.

connect 1) Call Kelly to congratulate her on her new job.
2) Call Aunt Gina to catch up.

Tips to maximize your Ph.ME! Plan include the following:

- Put genuine thought into what you want to be recorded in your heart and mind. If it's not meaningful when you think about it, don't write it.

- Write your goals in the present tense. Your brain does not know the difference between imaginary and real, so speak it into existence by speaking as if it's already real.

- Commit to writing down goals and dreams regularly, and keep your weekly, individual Ph.ME! card where you can see it. This will help you avoid making decisions that will lead you away from your goals.

- Commit to achieving what you write down and follow through—act!

- Write things down in detail—set a specific, clear visual of what you want to accomplish.

- Incorporate deadlines when applicable.

- Break down a larger goal into smaller, achievable steps. Creating a milestone and achieving it is a huge morale booster and can bring on even more determination to succeed.

Chapter Two

_____

WHAT IS THE PH.ME! PLAN?

*Decide what it is you want, write it down, review it constantly,
and each day do something that moves you toward those goals.*
~ Jack Canfield

BY WRITING THINGS DOWN
<u>THAT ARE IMPORTANT TO YOU</u>
OR MOTIVATE, CHALLENGE, INSPIRE,
EXCITE, OR CONNECT YOU TO OTHERS,
YOU ARE:

1 CREATING A STEP-BY-STEP ACTION PLAN.

CLARIFYING WHAT YOU WANT. **2**

3 IMPROVING THE 'ENCODING' PROCESS, WHICH INCREASES THE CHANCES OF INFORMATION BEING STORED FOR LATER.

42% MORE LIKELY TO ACHIEVE GOALS IF DONE REGULARLY. **4**

5 DEVEOPING A VISUAL CUE

BOOSTING MOTIVATION TO TAKE ACTION **6**

7 ABLE TO PROCESS VISUALS 60,000 TIMES FASTER THAN IF YOU HAD TO IMAGINE THEM.

ACTIVATING RIGHT AND LEFT-BRAIN HEMISPHERES STIMULATING A NEW REALM OF CONSCIOUSNESS WHICH OCCURS WHEN WRITING THINGS DOWN. **8**

We all have To-Do lists, whether written on a piece of paper or a sticky note, logged in our phones, or just etched in our minds. Those lists are usually things we *need* to do—not necessarily what we *want* to do—and, quite often, they don't lift our spirits or fulfill us mentally, physically, or spiritually.

Natural enrichment lies in the tasks we want to do—the stuff that's good for the soul. How do you get back to a life with more of that and incorporate it into your daily schedule? It is easier than you might think.

According to cell biologist Dr. Bruce Lipton, anything that comes into a person's life is because that person has an internal program that supports those things. Ninety-five percent of a person's life stems from programs developed in the first seven years. We have over seventy thousand thoughts a day, many harmful or repetitive because we default to the familiar.

In light of that, is reprogramming the subconscious possible? Yes.

How? Through repetition. That is, when we repeat behaviors, we create new *habits*, meaning we do it religiously.

When the mind eventually commits it to memory, as a normal conscious thought, the habit becomes automatic, and voilà—a new program.

A scientifically proven method[1] for achieving goals is to write[2] them down. Doing so improves the *encoding process*, in which

1 New Tech Northwest - The Psychology of Writing Down Goals - https://www.newtechnorthwest.com/the-psychology-of-writing-down-goals/
2 Forbes.com - Neuroscience Explains Why You Need to Write Down Your Goals if You Actually Want to Achieve Them by Mark Murphy -https://

information is relayed to the brain's hippocampus, where it decides whether to commit thoughts to short- or long-term memory. By engaging in the physical act of writing down ideas, the complex sensory information increases the chances of data being stored for later.

To further illustrate the concept of encoding, the *generation effect*, a well-studied memory phenomenon, can be shared. This phenomenon is described as one in which information is remembered better if generated from the mind rather than being read. Psychologists and educators have long embraced the value of mnemonic techniques: tools designed to help memory. Why? Because they work.[3]

In one study, psychologists analyzed the neural basis of the generation effect by showing participants one-word cues. Using an MRI, they examined the fundamental units of the brain and nervous system, specifically investigating the cells responsible for receiving sensory input from external forces. During encoding, some study participants wrote down synonyms for the word cues. Compared to reading the words alone, those who wrote them down had a significantly higher performance for later recalling them.

According to Dr. Bruce Lipton, author of *The Biology of Belief: Unleashing the Power of Consciousness, Matter & Miracles*, and an American developmental biologist most known for his views and studies of epigenetics, "Perception is awareness shaped by

www.forbes.com/sites/markmurphy/2018/04/15/neuroscience-explains-why-you-need-to-write-down-your-goals-if-you-actually-want-to-achieve-them/?sh=45948df87905

3 Dr. Bruce Lipton - author of The Biology of Belief: Unleashing the Power of Consciousness. - https://www.brucelipton.com/

beliefs. Beliefs 'control' perception. Rewrite beliefs, and you rewrite perception. Rewrite perception, and you rewrite genes and behavior."

You may be wondering: *Can I consciously and purposefully create the life I want to live?* The answer is yes.

Many people are living a life of frustration, feeling that what exists is not what they want, and they do not understand why these disharmonies continue surfacing. Anyone struggling with understanding why certain circumstances repeat would be helped by knowing the world is made up of energy. By understanding this concept, one can then recognize the way our early conditioning shapes that energy, and how we, as individuals, hang on to old beliefs that keep us stuck in the repetition of undesirable circumstances

To explore this further, much of what shapes our lives comes from our subconscious mind, programming from early childhood, our family, and our culture. So, while your conscious mind wants one thing, the subconscious mind is programmed to deliver another. By clarifying what you want, stimulating a whole new realm of consciousness, creating a plan, and developing visual cues regularly, it *is* possible to create the life you want.

The exciting part is this: It is not the outside world that limits our happiness or the pursuit of our goals and dreams. Each person can make these changes. And each individual can make dreams become reality simply with the courage to pursue them.

When you write things down, you confidently make an action plan and clarify what you want. You also provide yourself with a visual cue to ensure your desires and goals are at the top of your mind. Taken a step further, you can assign a date to your goal and break it down into steps; this is your plan. Backed by action, any dream can become a reality.

Chapter Three

_____

WHAT IS YOUR LIFE-CHANGING WORD?

Happiness is a choice.

~ Valerie Bertinelli

Are you ready to introduce something to your life that is a game-changer? Great!

Years ago, I read a book called *One Word That Will Change Your Life*. The title is ridiculously accurate because it seriously changed my life. I learned about it in my church's Small Group (a Christian book club). We discussed the book in one of our sessions and then made it our homework to choose our one word.

The concept is to select a word that encompasses what you want to increase or improve in your life, and therefore the word brings you a sense of focus. It should encapsulate who and how you want to be; by focusing on that word, your thoughts and actions will propel you toward your goal.

Following this practice for the last five years, I have found the most empowering and life-changing words have chosen me. If you devote the space for your one word with thought, prayers, or whatever speaks to you, it will come to you. When I first read the book, I was going through a reflective period of life, and I had a lot of doubt that maybe I wasn't meant to have the type of joy and happiness that many people around me seemed to have.

I wondered if maybe I had simply chosen the wrong path; therefore, I was stuck with the type of life portrayed in *Bridget Jones's Diary*. You know, the "hard-working girl who tries hard at life but always seems to fall short in categories where one would prefer not to fall short." These thoughts kept me up at night, wondering how things may have looked had I chosen something else or someone else.

I can honestly say that all that contemplation was unhealthy for me. Because, as most of us realize, what we focus on keeps coming back to us. Over-analyzing the many decisions I'd made and replaying my feelings were precisely what *not* to do!

One thing my friends and family have always said about me is that I am incredibly positive and full of hope. That is who I am to the core and one thing I like about myself. After much thought, my first chosen word was TRUST. I've had some challenges with trusting—myself, my decision-making, others, and their intentions—throughout my life. In general, I make others earn my trust before I extend it freely. So TRUST seemed like a great starter word.

After each member of our small group had chosen their word, my friend Georgia—we call her GA—had magnets made, featuring each word, and gave them to us as gifts, reminders of what we were to focus on that year. Because of my newfound focus, I saw the word trust a lot in everyday life, which made me recognize its significance in my world.

When I met new people, I took note of whether I felt I could trust them early on or if trusting them would take some time. Placing a great deal of attention on this word allowed me to grow immensely in the area in which I wanted growth. It changed what I was bringing into my life.

During that time, I prayed and asked God to bring me situations in which I would be required to trust. Some situations weren't easy, but they all were exactly what I needed and very rewarding in the long run.

I encourage you to identify your one word. Imagine what in your life you want or need to change. Think about it, pray, talk to your close friends, jot things down when they come across your mind, and then go back and look at those notes and see if they spark anything. Meditate, go for jogs, or sit in silence. I promise you if you ask your word to make itself known, it will. And you will know when it does because it will feel like a major epiphany.

Once your word chooses you, write it in your new Ph.ME! Plan, on your Ph. ME! card, or someplace you can see it regularly. Each time I have chosen a new word, or it has chosen me, I receive something that has my word on it. The year after I had TRUST, the word BELIEVE chose me. I will tell you that after I learned to trust a little more freely, I finally felt great about where I was in life and how I was impacting others. I met my person, and I was asked to lead a divorce recovery group so that I could use my difficult situation from years before to help others. I felt stable in my career, owned a beautiful home, thrived financially, captained my tennis team, and cultivated abundant friendships.

The best part was that I trusted in it all. Even though I trusted in God and others, I still struggled now and again, believing it was all meant for me and meant to last. Feeling this way showed me that working to fill my cup wasn't just a one-and-done thing. It was going to be a lifelong process, but a good one. Then, one day it hit me—BELIEVE was my next word. I immediately texted several friends with just that word and quickly received responses like, "Yes!" or "OMG, that's perfect for you!" And it was.

Shortly after assigning myself this empowering word for the year, I remembered the story of Melanie Oudin. Melanie was a seventeen-year-old tennis player from Marietta, Georgia, who had the word BELIEVE on her tennis shoes as a constant reminder that even when fear is overwhelming, you should believe. Melanie, an unseeded player, wound up pulling off four upsets, including beating out well-known tennis superstar Maria Sharapova and gracing the U.S. Open quarterfinals, being the youngest quarterfinalist since Serena Williams in 1999. She became a tennis sensation overnight and gave many people a reason to believe.

Being a tennis player myself, I was particularly influenced by Melanie's story. In particular, I could relate to how her love of tennis began by hitting a tennis ball against the garage of her house. I had done the same thing as a kid. To this day, being on a tennis court is one of my happy places. Now, my tennis abilities are nowhere close to Melanie's, but I imagine she and

I share the same A-game level of belief. And, by the way, if you are currently humming Journey's "Don't Stop Believing" right about now, I totally get it.

Melanie's story of persevering through difficult situations inspired me to keep going and believe. She has often shared stories of going through devastating losses, but she learned from them. Even though she didn't win the 2009 U.S. Open title, she still came out a winner with an incredible singles grand-slam experience, a surplus of media and sponsor opportunities, and a hard-fought journey that led her to a 2011 grand-slam win, with doubles partner Jack Sock.

From all of this, I realized that if I continued to believe in my own goals and dreams and always moved toward them, I would be a winner too.

After BELIEVE, I took the year off from my one word. That year, I lost a little focus on mastering my life. I had taken a major risk—I uprooted my secure, stable, organized, happy life to head to another state, planning to become engaged. After two years of trying my best to make that relationship work, I had to face the reality of it not being the right fit. I knew that ending the relationship meant I would be starting over in life. *Starting over* as in moving back to Georgia, finding a new job, a new home, and starting from almost scratch on furnishing that home, as I had sold just about everything I owned.

My ultimate indicator that this would be hard was that I did not even own a coffee maker. That was the equivalent of "this is going to sting!" And that scared the absolute hell out of me. Being in my forties and starting over, with no coffee maker even?! I can think of hundreds of less painful things to do, but I was faced with this one. And an undercaffeinated me is not a good me. It was here that I met a significant challenge.

After a lot of praying, I realized starting over was the only way to get back my positive, hopeful self. Believe me—yes, believe, and not in a Melanie Oudin way!—that girl was *gone!* But I wanted her back, and I just had no idea how to do it.

Shortly before I had officially decided to move back to Georgia and start my life over, I had a little sit-down with God and told Him that I was just done and tired of trying and that if He needed me, He should go ahead and wrap things up for me down here on Earth. Yeah, it was bad. After that chat, I received a call from my doctor alerting me that she noticed something questionable on my recent exam. Yep, that was it. I knew it right then. I was about to be told that I had cancer and would be starting chemo, radiation, and a battle that I was terrified to take, and it might even have been the end of the road for me.

On the morning of my appointment, I sat in the exam room waiting for the doctor to come in to insert some extremely large—what I can only describe as gardening —tools into my body, I decided to pray.

My prayer was something like this:

> *God, I'm scared. I know I asked for this, and I know you heard me because you always do. I need you to hold my hand through this entire journey, whatever you're going to make it be. But also, I want you to know that even though I am afraid of starting over, I will do it if you will just let me*

live. And if you let me live—yes, I'm negotiating with You like I've done a hundred times and probably even said the words 'I'll never ask for anything again'—I promise to live as you've never seen anyone do before. I realize now that living an amazing life is what I really want, and giving up is not me!

I left the doctor's office that morning, genuinely wondering what the outcome would be, but mostly I expected a phone call with awful news. I hopped in my car, headed off to Georgia for a work trip, and did my best to put the harmful thoughts out of my mind. My seven-hour drive consisted of the sky letting loose the sideways-type rain and my being surrounded by monstrous semis blowing by, forcing massive amounts of water over my windshield every few seconds. I tried my best to maintain control of my car.

Around 9:00 p.m., as I was driving in the blackness, I realized that, for the first time during the drive, I had a whole minute where I was not inches away from huge trucks whizzing by, nearly blasting me off the road. In that split-second of realization, I saw two large spotlights appear in my rearview mirror, which, on impact, left me helpless and at the mercy of God. It was His call now.

At that moment, I lost complete control of my car. An SUV had slammed into the back of my car, forcing me to immediately rotate horizontally into the left lane, the same one where semis had been rushing by me the entire night. My car swirled around on the highway. As it did, I will never forget, right at that moment I fully accepted that my life was over and I was about to die.

I will never know how long the actual incident lasted, but I eventually made it to the side of the road. I was in the dark, alone and in silence, shaking and wondering what the hell had just happened. All I knew was that I was alive, miraculously alive, but alive.

The next day, I shared my story with my Small Group, and one of them replied with these poetic words. Her words, and I quote, were, "Girl, your angels were with you yesterday!"

She was closer to the truth than she knew. My mom, my Nana, my Poppi, my grandmother, my friend Robin, my former cats, the lovebird that died when I was thirteen, the two mice I bought my brother for his birthday when I was fourteen—they were *all* with me, lifting me out of that flipping mess. And they all gave me what I wanted: a chance to *live*.

If you're curious, the doctor's office called me back several days later to tell me that my results were clear and I did not have cancer. That was the most enormous sigh of relief I have ever let out, let me tell you. But the message I received loud and clear from that day is this: If you put the message out there, God hears you. But also, *you* hear *you*. The power of your spoken and written words is beyond powerful. Remember that, and use words to bring into your life what you truly want and not what you feel you should settle for because you're afraid to go after what you want.

So, I wonder if you can guess what my next word was for that following year. Do you think you know? Did you guess *LIVE?* If so, you nailed it!

And ever since that word has chosen me, I do my best to make the most of every day that I'm upright. Do I slip and get lazy on some days? Sure—but I do my best to point out the positive in any situation, regardless of how daunting it may seem. I owe it to myself, and I don't plan to let myself down again.

So, I want to know, what is your one word?

Do you lack adventure in your life? Are you someone who doesn't take risks, so you possibly miss out on great opportunities and wonder just *what if?* Do you need to incorporate bravery into your life to enable you to try new things? What about balance, abundance, rest, growth, or surrender—do any of these words sound impactful to you?

Think about what you want more of in your life that would affect your entire well-being, success, and relationships. Then put it aside. That's when the game-changing word will appear. I guarantee it.

Chapter Four

ARE YOU CHASING YOUR DREAMS AND GOALS?

Not everyone will understand your journey. That's fine.
It's not their journey to make sense of. It's yours.
~ Zero Dean

First things first: Have you determined your dreams in life and established goals for yourself? If you have, that's great! Are you actively chasing them down? Because one very important truth to note is that your dreams don't chase you. So if you have one, and it keeps you up at night, and you just wonder what it will be like when it comes true, well, get ready to run it down.

Planning your dreams and writing down your goals are crucial for a happy, healthy, productive, fulfilling life. I've always heard that you should dream big dreams—the bigger, the better. I'm talking so big, you may even laugh at them because they seem so over the top. But, if they weren't so wild and exhilarating to think about, then they probably wouldn't be called *dreams* now, would they? They'd be called something more ordinary, like realistic expectations.

Why shouldn't we dream about slightly scary things? What pushes us out of our comfort zones or seems impossible can actually turn out to be motivating and challenging. And to state the obvious, they are our dreams and no one else's, so it shouldn't matter what others think about *our* dreams. If they don't understand or agree with them, that's completely fine. Do you know why? Because that dream is in your heart, not theirs. So the sky should be the limit.

We have one life—one. Isn't it in our best interest to focus on the absolute most exciting dreams ever, the ones that make us smile without knowing it and give us chills when we contemplate what it will be like when they come true? Seriously, let's think about this. We only have one go-round in life. And, as we all know, time often slips by quicker than we'd like.

Someone once called me a dreamer, but they meant it negatively. Being the positive person I am, I chose to hear it as a compliment and said thanks.

I started to think about the opposite of a dreamer. I felt sad thinking about what type of person that must be. Many people are self-proclaimed realists, and that's all well and good. But even a realist can dream. Anyone can dream. Everyone should want to dream. Dreaming prompts growth and keeps us moving in life, looking forward to each day and opening our eyes to the possibility of a new vision coming to fruition.

I am sure you have heard about visualization boards. For obvious reasons, writing down your dreams and goals is complemented by a vision board. When you write down your dreams and goals, be specific. These are your dreams and goals; only *you* know the details of these precious thoughts. Write down every little detail so you can see it as clearly as if it were in front of you, staring into your soul.

I'll give you an example. One of my dreams is to have a beach house. I know what it looks like because I have dreamed about it so many times. It has a glorious, open-plan kitchen that is primarily white with touches of navy blue on various cabinets, white marble countertops with tiny gray specks, and gold hardware. It has a massive island in the center where loads of family and friends can gather. The kitchen opens up to the living room, which opens up to the deck overlooking the ocean where my loved ones spend quality time together—my No. 1 love language, by the way.

My beach house encompasses togetherness at its finest. I've envisioned lots of laughing, talking, and being with loved ones so often, I can almost hear the actual conversations if I think about it long enough. Even the thought of it now, as I am writing, brings the biggest smile to my face because I know that it will come true someday. I write this dream down often, which truly brings happiness to my day.

Goals are very similar. If you are a child, why would you hope for a B on a test when what you really want is an A? The same should be true for adults when we write down our goals. Are you striving to be a manager at your company, or is what you really want to be the vice president? If being the V.P. would make you happier, then, by all means, write down those two letters on the Dreams + Goals line of your Ph.ME! card. Done and done! Then start preparing for that role, not the one you feel isn't as exciting or worth pursuing but feels doable. Goals and dreams aren't about doable. Doable is easy, doable doesn't challenge you, and doable sure as heck doesn't excite you!

Chapter Five

HOW ARE YOU PRACTICING WEEKLY SELF-CARE?

I have come to believe that caring for
myself is not self-indulgence.
It is self-preservation...

~ Audre Lorde

A Burst of Light and Other Essays

We often think self-care is easy to incorporate into daily life, but it usually proves to be difficult.

Most of us are quite familiar with practices that soothe our soul, energize, inspire, or relax and center us. But many times, as the result of a physically or mentally exhausting day or becoming sidetracked with trivial distractions, we put our self-care at the bottom of our list. Self-care is vital for our overall state of being, yet we set it aside so quickly. Activities that fuel self-care are often the most enjoyable and relaxing. Yet, they're still easily ignored.

I've found one way to raise my spirits is to take a long walk or hike, when I can clear my head and enjoy the benefits of being in nature. I also listen to podcasts or find YouTube videos to learn hobbies or skills that are on my list. I make time to connect with friends or family. My mind never shuts down, so I find that meditating is excellent for self-care too.

I love playing tennis and find that I am at my happiest when I'm on a tennis court. I also find that I fulfill my self-care when I'm doing things to nurture my relationship with God. Oddly enough, when I'm playing tennis, it makes me feel closer to God. You might think, "How can tennis get you close to God?" And, no, it's not when people yell, "Lord Jesus, help me hit the freaking ball!" The way I look at it is I don't think it's possible to have that much fun, do something I enjoy, release all of my daily worries, and not feel like it's a gift from God. So there you go, tennis and God. It is what it is.

Other things that make me feel like I'm checking off boxes for self-care are setting aside a night by myself where I can watch movies or read books that literally make me laugh out loud. I love to laugh, so I take any opportunity I have to do that. I also love watching a good horror flick, but about a year ago, I decided those weren't adding to my positive self-talk or helping me get quality sleep. So I traded in Ted Bundy for Ted Lasso—about 80 percent of the time, anyway.

Who in your life makes you smile, laugh, and feel great about yourself, just as you are? Jot down those names on the line for self-care. They are crucial for this. Make time for these people often.

When I'm down, the first person I call is my boyfriend or one of my best friends. I know that my boyfriend will make me laugh, and he will have some good nuggets of advice. But the laughing is what I'm really hoping he'll finish the "talk me off the ledge" chat with. Laughing is essential for well-being and is absolutely part of self-care!

- Laughter protects the heart by improving blood vessels' function and increasing blood flow, which can help protect against heart attack and other cardiovascular issues.

- Laughter reduces stress chemicals in your brain and increases immune cells and infection-fighting antibodies, thus improving disease resistance.

- Laughter eases anxiety and tension and strengthens resilience.

- Negative thoughts manifest into chemical reactions that bring about stress, which decreases immunity. Alternatively, positive thoughts—and laughter— can release neuropeptides that help fight stress and potentially more severe illnesses.

- Laughter enhances the intake of oxygen-rich air; stimulates the heart, lungs, and muscles; and increases endorphins released by the brain.

A year ago, I started a gluten-free diet. I feel amazing. This new way of eating has been a life changer. I've always heard people talk about how it includes transformative healing elements. I guess I was just being stubborn and didn't want to give up pizza, the yummy bread they serve at restaurants, and crackers with cheese. I know all you gluten-free people out there are probably saying: *But you can still have those things!* It just took me a while to realize that gluten-free pizza doesn't have to be a big, fat letdown. The results have been well worth eliminating wheat-based pizza. The joint pain I occasionally suffer due to gluten is gone. By the way, gluten-free Oreos are flipping amazing. And, yes, those are good for my self-care too.

By using the Ph.ME! Plan, and specifically writing down how I'd like to incorporate self-care into my week in the space provided on the card, I can say my level of self-care has increased. The bottom line is finding ways to boost your health and happiness, which doesn't always have to cost money.

Chapter Six

WHAT IS YOUR POSITIVE AFFIRMATION FOR THE WEEK?

Let your dreams be bigger than your fears and
your actions be louder than your words.

~ Anonymous

Live life—don't just exist!

This phrase alone is enough to stop me in my tracks and set me straight. It's almost a dare to me. Whenever I hear myself read aloud the words from a note I've written to myself, it gets me back on track. I ask myself if I am genuinely living life or if I am just coasting through the week.

Here are some other powerful affirmations:

- *I am worthy—exactly as I am.*

- *I have enough, and I am enough.*

- *I will achieve my goals by taking one step at a time.*

- *I am strong, and I am capable.*

- *If you can't beat fear, do it scared.*

- *I can do all things through Christ, who strengthens me.* ~ Philippians 4:13, King James Version

- *I can do anything I set my mind to.*

- *"I choose to make the rest of my life the best of my life."* ~ Louise Hay

- *"The best preparation for tomorrow is doing your best today."* ~ H. Jackson Brown Jr.

What words inspire you to take steps forward and spread positivity or give you the kickstart you need to grab life by its rays of sunshine and charge full steam ahead?

I don't know about you, but for me, the affirmations that keep me going steadily in the right direction vary from week to week. I typically latch on to ones that keep me optimistic and proud about where I am in life and what I accomplish. There are always those weeks when I look around, or inward, and think I haven't done enough with my life. So, a specific affirmation may serve me better in that regard. Something like this one:

I am exactly where I am meant to be.

Admittedly, there are weeks when I feel beaten down and almost as if I can't do anything right. Those weeks are beyond frustrating, but the worst feeling is to wish for those days to be behind you quickly. I don't want to wish time away because with that go opportunities for happiness, growth, adventure, and possibly moments you may never have the chance to experience again. Have you ever had one of those weeks? What would be your go-to affirmation during a week like that?

I am a lover of quotes. One of my habits, if I'm feeling down or discouraged, is to go on Pinterest and look for positive quotes in whatever category is challenging me. I typically find a few dozen that get me back to my usual, optimistic, hopeful self.

> *Don't look for your dreams to become true;*
> *look to become true to your dreams.*
>   ~ Michael Bernard Beckwith.

Whatever your words for the week are, remember this: Your self-talk is critical to who you are—I mean who you are to the very core. How do you want others to speak to you? How would you like others to talk to your spouse, best friend, or child?

Exactly. So choose your weekly written affirmations very wisely.

Those words should be the match that lights your soul on fire!

Chapter Seven

WHAT WOULD YOU LIKE TO LEARN?

If you are not willing to learn, no one can help you.
If you are determined to learn, no one can stop you.

~ Zig Ziglar

Just the other day, someone told me about an icebreaker question he'd had in a meeting that was two-fold. The first part was, "What is something you can now do that you didn't know how to do this time last year?" The second part was, "What do you hope you will be able to say about this year if you are asked that question a year from now?"

As an adult, acquiring new skills can be exciting. Another way to learn is by looking at situations in your life that didn't go as planned and viewing them as opportunities to make different, in some cases, better decisions. It's all about growing! Not long ago, a pandemic was the guiding factor, with frequent "stay at home" mandates and occasional periods of fear when a new strand of the virus surfaced. Those slow-downs for many were a blessing, as they provided more time than we previously had to explore genuine interests.

Like many others, I lost my job during the height of the pandemic. It all made sense, so I wasn't stunned when it happened. But it did provide a lot of anxiety for someone who is always planning and organized. Suddenly I was engulfed in a situation where I was unsure of a lot, but it gave me more time to broaden my skill set and learn things I had always wanted to know.

As I was scouring the internet and job boards, looking at roles that interested me, I noticed skills I was lacking. It seemed as if companies were looking to hire the knowledge and expertise of two people in one. Again—this was understandable because many companies had also been severely affected by the pandemic and the loss of business. So what used to be marketing-only roles now appeared to be marketing, graphic design, *and* web design. Initially, it was a little daunting, but I took it on as a challenge! I used my downtime to teach myself how to build and design websites and fine-tune my graphic design skills.

Answering the question about what I know now that I didn't a year ago is easy. I now know my way around several graphic design software programs and can build and manage websites. Not only can I quickly navigate them, but I enjoy it. As I developed my creative skills even further, I incorporated them into real-time projects, which opened doors for new opportunities and enabled me to design and write a book and create a product using new software tools. I also applied these skills to obtain a role on the board of a nonprofit organization as their marketing director and was able to support a very worthwhile cause called the *I AM ENOUGH movement.*

Looking back at how I survived the two years of isolation, uncertainty, and pressure that the pandemic provided, I can honestly say that I am proud of what I learned and accomplished. If you were to take inventory of how you came out on the other side, could you say the same? If you can, that's great. If not, what would you like to change *today?* Because if you are reading this book, I imagine you are seeking solutions to improve your life.

> *Always keep learning. It keeps you young.*
> ~ Patty Berg

Sometimes I wish I could go back to college and retake courses, join different clubs, get more involved in as many organizations as physically possible, or have another chance to chat with my brilliant professors. Now that I am an adult and fully know where my interests and strengths lie, I would have most likely taken a completely different course load, thereby altering my path. And I would have asked more questions, researched more, and daydreamed more about how all that knowledge could one day transform my life. I loved college and did well while there; but looking back, I don't think I realized what a crazy ridiculous opportunity I had right at my fingertips.

In the same vein, I find it funny how many of us, now as adults, would jump at the chance to tell our young adult selves things that would impact us. If you'd asked me when I was younger my thoughts on seeking additional opportunities on top of my workload in college, I probably would have had an entirely different answer. Today, I look at learning as such an incredible gift in life and a chance to improve myself.

I often think back to being young and asking my mom how to spell certain words. Her answer baffled me. She would always tell me to look it up. Here I am thinking, "I just asked you how to spell it; surely I can't look it up if I don't know how to spell it!?" But she was right.

That constant curiosity of wanting to know led me to win the school spelling bee in sixth grade. I made it all the way to the county fair and took second place. Yes, second—as in, the person right after the winner. It was a devastating loss. I will never forget the word that I misspelled. After learning how to spell words I didn't even know the meaning of and studying for weeks on end, I lost attempting to spell the word *gracious*. Seriously? Gracious?! I *am* gracious by every definition of the darn word. And in all fairness, I think if everyone spelled it with a T instead of a C, things would be just fine in the world.

Nonetheless, it was a lesson I learned the hard way: to keep trying; great things come to second-place winners too. But I was a winner in my own right because I was seeking excellence, and I learned a heck of a lot of other things throughout my journey. And the pursuit of excellence partnered with quality time with someone you love, which in my case was my mother, was equally as much of a win. Coincidentally, to this day, I am an excellent speller, and I never misspell *gracious*. Even though I giggle a little bit because I can still picture myself many years ago—this little bitty girl standing on stage in front of what felt like hundreds of people spelling gracious with a T. We win some, we lose some— am I right? My mom treated me to an enormous ice cream cone that day, by the way. So, yes, I was pretty much a winner.

I challenge everyone to learn regularly. What interests you? What would make you a better partner or friend or employee? Think of something you wish you could do but think it's too late to learn. Challenge your belief—what's one step you could take toward acquiring that skill? It is never too late to learn.

Did you know:

- Julia Child began her culinary studies when she was nearly forty, with her first cookbook published a decade later, ultimately leading her to become a world-renowned celebrity chef.

- Vera Wang wanted to be an Olympic figure skater but failed to join the team. At age forty, she designed her first gown: her own wedding dress. Today she is one of the world's most admired designers in fashion.

- Heard of McDonald's? Ray Kroc cofounded his burger franchise with the McDonald brothers when he was fifty-two, and he bought it outright from them at fifty-nine, turning it into the multi-billion dollar endeavor it is today.

- Momofuku Ando, inventor of instant ramen noodles, created this phenomenon in 1958 when he was forty-eight.

My point is this, friends: What are you waiting for? What do you want to learn, do, experience, conquer, and master?

A boyfriend of mine many years ago gave me a birthday card intended for a child. I looked at it and thought: *Why on earth did he get me a kid's card?! I know I don't necessarily look my age, but I certainly don't look like a six-year-old.* But what he told me sticks with me to this day. He told me to never stop looking at the world through a child's eyes. That means never stop wondering, never stop being fascinated or curious about how something works or why something is the way it is.

Remember when you were a kid and had questions about absolutely everything? Do you remember having the ability to cry over something one second and, five minutes later, being so wrapped up in something else that you had forgotten all about the earlier catastrophe? Today, even though you are no longer a child, consider applying that childlike view and curiosity to learn; seek answers and knowledge and go after all the world has to offer.

Along this path of discovery, if you wind up feeling nostalgic about your childhood as you reminisce, that is just a bonus. Learn to allow yourself to process something painful and then let it go so you can get back to living your amazing life. And let me tell you, don't take that feeling for granted—embrace it.

Chapter Eight

ARE YOU ACTIVELY PURSUING NEW SKILLS AND HOBBIES?

Hobbies are not just for passing the time.
It is a way for your soul to recharge.

~ anonymous

Hobbies enrich our lives, regardless of whether they require physical activity or mental alertness or tapping into a creative side. They are enjoyable because we choose them. Some hobbies can even be considered skills. Think about something you've wanted to try—such as photography, painting, writing, chalk painting, calligraphy, pickleball, Pilates, or cycling.

Now, imagine picking up a hobby and becoming so good at it that you start receiving compliments repeatedly on the finished product. Now consider people asking to commission some of your artwork for money—it could happen. Next, you are working on your website or an Etsy shop, and the activity you started off doing because you wanted to learn something new has become a revenue generator. Wow, go you! You're still enjoying taking photos or creating art, but you've learned something that has advanced your education *and* your finances.

I typically write a list on my Ph.ME! Plan of the things I want to get involved in. I've always had a creative mind. From the time I was a child, I have been asking questions. As an adult, I'm still asking them. I'm curious, and life is full of fascinating phenomena that I want to know more about and understand.

Think about the last time you moved to a new city, started a new job, or began dating someone new. What were some of your first acts and experiences? I'm guessing that you discovered where your new coffee shop and grocery store were located if you moved. Or you taught yourself how to properly hang pictures on the wall to avoid hammering in a nail eight times before getting it right while praying no one ever takes the artwork down for fear of seeing your connect-the-dots of nail holes. If you started a new job, maybe you studied the nuances of the company and discovered the most efficient route to your workplace. If you started dating someone new, I'll bet you researched the fun, new local hot spots; activities you could do together; or tourist attractions in your city. No matter the circumstance, what they all have in common is you probably learned a lot of new things.

I want you to recall the last significant thing you learned:

- How did you feel afterward?

- Did you build on that skill or hobby?

- How has that enriched your life?

- Did you make new friends because of it?

- Did it help you land your dream job?

- Did it help you fulfill a dream?

- Did it help you attain a goal or allow you to cross something off of your bucket list?

- Did that new hobby give you something to look forward to each week?

People often say that everything we do builds off something else, and I believe that. Looking back at new hobbies and skills I've added to my life each year makes me feel a tremendous sense of accomplishment—and I feel proud that I strive to be the best version of myself.

In the past two years, I have learned my way around a few creative software programs rather well. Because of that new knowledge, I got my dream job, furthering my career. I can cross an item off my bucket list. The bucket list item is writing this book and creating this product. Not that I couldn't do that without knowing the software programs, but because I took the time to educate myself and pursued training, I was able to design the product and book *myself*. Doing that allowed me to feel an even deeper connection to the development of the product and my mission of sharing something with others that is important to me.

My point is this: Never underestimate the power of learning new skills and hobbies and what they can do for you in many areas of your life. Take this as a challenge to see what new software program you can learn, or go online and take a course on how to do voiceovers, or find a local Chamber of Commerce that hosts Toastmaster sessions and master public speaking.

Activities such as these propel you forward in the professional world and give you more confidence.

Are you a quiet person who wishes you could stand out in a crowd and maybe meet the person of your dreams? Are you someone who would love to have more business connections? Do you feel it would benefit you to be better at making small talk?

There are many great sayings about comfort zones:

> *Step so far outside your comfort zone*
> *that you forget how to get back.*
>
> ~ unknown

> *If it doesn't challenge you, it doesn't change you.*
>
> ~ unknown

> *Do one thing every day that scares you.*
>
> ~ Eleanor Roosevelt

> *A comfort zone is a beautiful place, but nothing ever grows there.*
>
> ~ unknown

As many of us seriously dislike being displaced from our comfort zone, it is very healthy and beneficial to do so. If you were always in your bubble, safe and secure, how would you ever learn new things, meet new people, or be exposed to life-changing moments? It's certainly worth a shot. Give it a try. If you escape unharmed and walk away with a new skill or friend, it might be worth doing over and over, wouldn't you say?

Think back to when you were a child. Did your parents constantly push or encourage you to participate in new sports or activities? To try soccer, softball, art, gymnastics, playing piano, writing stories, cooking . . . the list goes on. Most of the time, I liked learning new things and getting involved, with only rare occasions when I realized the activity wouldn't last longer than a season. But at least I found out rather than wondered about it. Essentially, my parents exposed me to things I needed to explore. Now, as adults, we should be able to do that ourselves.

It's not always easy, and sometimes we get busy, but that's the purpose of the Ph.ME! Plan. Writing these things down and creating a visual reminder will help you follow through with the items on your list. I would venture to say that, along the way, you will discover things that you are particularly good at too.

Chapter Nine

_____

DO YOU GIVE AS OFTEN AS YOU WOULD LIKE?

The best and most beautiful things in this world
cannot be seen or even heard but must be felt with the heart.
~ Helen Keller

Surely you have heard about the book *The Five Love Languages* by Gary D. Chapman. If you haven't, here is a brief overview. Different people have different personalities, so it makes sense that everyone would give and receive love in different ways. The five different Love Languages are:

- Acts of Service: An act of kindness that helps another

- Giving Gifts: Tangible tokens of affection

- Physical Touch: A touch that reflects your thoughtfulness and affection

- Quality Time: Undivided attention spent with someone you care about

- Words of Affirmation: Verbal compliments that express your love and appreciation for someone

When you imagine giving, what does that look like to you? How would it look viewed through the lens of one of the five love languages?

Here's an example that may clarify making the most of your giving. My father is in his eighties and lives in another state. As he's gotten older, I've felt more challenged to find gifts that he will enjoy. Several years ago, he told me that if I wanted to get him a gift, my time was what he wanted the most. Well, there you go. It can't get any easier than someone telling you exactly what they want.

Since then, I've made an effort to call him as often as possible to fill him in on the details of my tennis match or tell him about the project I've got going on at work, and sometimes we chat about the latest movie we've seen. Each time I call, his first question is, "Where are you driving now, honey?" He knows I'm usually leaving work, headed to tennis, or out on a walk when I call. But it's that uninterrupted time I have with him that we both value so much. To him and me, that is a gift, showing our love to each other.

So giving isn't always about writing a check to someone you don't know; it can be very much about giving of yourself to someone you do know. And we should be aware of what those people require to feel loved.

Recently I met a woman who told me about her unique way of tithing. Her method of giving is to send two things a week to someone in her family. Sometimes it's flowers, other times a card with a $20 bill, and sometimes a little present that may have cost her $5.00. Regardless of what it is, she knows it will bring a smile to that person's face.

I asked if she ever felt God's timing played a role in this random act of kindness. She told me that she often felt God directing her on who to send to and what to send. Then she said that was her way of knowing it was the perfect way for her to tithe and give to others.

In addition to giving to those we know, now, more than ever, it's important to give to others. Giving can take a variety of forms. Our world has drastically changed over the past couple of years, and life has become more complicated. Our world has drastically changed since the pandemic. For many people, those feelings of anxiety, fear, and uncertainty linger. Many people have held on to the emotions tied to the dire importance of helping others in need at that time.

A fair amount of getting through similar uncertain circumstances can be managed by looking inward to discover our strengths. What qualities do you possess that could benefit someone else in a small way or enough to change their life?

My day-to-day personality is easy-going, and I do not enjoy arguing, nor do I revel in confrontation. However, recognizing the Scorpio in myself, I do find when I see someone else needing protection, I will step up to help them. I believe that is why others have always told me they think I am strong, even when I don't see it myself. I fight for others because I know I can.

With age, I have learned how truly blessed I am in life. I have an overabundance of comfort in life that so many others don't have. I am lucky to have an inner confidence that helps me stand tall daily. I am fortunate to have a phenomenal support system of friends and family. I am blessed to have a heightened level of positivity with me 99 percent of the time. And, for the 1 percent of the time it is not, others know me well enough to remind me it's still there.

When I talk about giving, much of it relates to helping someone else find the hope they need to keep pursuing a dream, a belief that they are worthy of love or a promotion, or whatever else in their heart seems a bit too far away.

Do you know anyone who doubts that they are worthy of a soulmate?

Do you know anyone who is out of work or miserable in their current role and lacks a skill you have?

Do you know someone elderly who is lonely and would benefit significantly from an hour-long phone conversation that you could easily fulfill on your commute to or from work?

Do you have a friend with a child doing a fundraiser whose confidence would be greatly boosted by your $10 donation?

Are you a part of an organization that could benefit from your skills?

Any of these things are considered giving.

Giving also ties in with connections that are crucial for having a happy, fulfilling life. Giving leads to so much more than just doing something nice for someone else in that moment. Giving changes lives.

Parents who teach their children the importance of giving set them up for a lifetime of awareness of others' needs and feelings. Have you ever given something to someone that made them so happy, and you just felt incredible joy yourself? Imagine the feeling you would get from making that a regular occurrence.

That is why filling in the Giving space on your Ph.ME! card will become such an essential part of your week. Giving unifies groups and communities, and giving makes people stronger. It is the undiscovered superpower, and it is infectious and continues far beyond that moment. Giving is far more than money; it is sharing resources and dedicating your time to someone. Giving is one of the most precious gifts there is.

As we work to create light for others,
we naturally light our own way.
~ Mary Anne Radmacher

Chapter Ten

ARE YOU NURTURING YOUR RELATIONSHIPS?

If you want a relationship that looks and feels like the most amazing thing on earth, you need to treat it like it is the most amazing thing on earth.

~ Akanshya Chand

Several years ago, I went to a funeral for my close friend's grandmother. I had met Lala maybe only twice, but knowing how important she was to Britt and Britt's mom, Marti, I wanted to be there. One thing that stood out to me was the number of people there. Even more noticeable was the number of people genuinely moved by her passing. It was easy to see this woman had made a tremendous impact on the lives of many.

I felt such emotion from everyone there. I told Marti it profoundly affected me and was life-changing. From that day forward, I realized when it's my turn to be the *guest of honor*, I want a church filled with people I inspired and who felt truly loved by me. I want to create a life and relationships filled with people for whom I did maybe only one small thing, but it was enough to make a massive, or even small but meaningful, difference in their lives.

There's so much that we all want out of life. I realized my deepest desire is to love people and feel their love for me. But those circumstances don't arise without effort; they develop out of being there for people, caring about them, and showing them they matter.

During the stay-at-home mandates during the height of the pandemic, I recognized the desire to connect with others was a significant quality I wanted in my life. But so many of us take connection for granted, and I know I definitely have.

Connection with others can make you feel whole, accepted, valued, and loved. Whether you realize it or not, connecting is crucial to your existence. It is common knowledge that healthy relationships and social support systems are integral to lifelong wellness, and these interactions begin in early childhood.

So I wondered about people who are alone and don't have many others to connect with daily or weekly. My dad was one. He's eighty-six, lives alone, and is nearly six hours away, making regular visits more difficult. Although phone calls are nice and certainly something I have ramped up over the years with him, there truly is nothing better than an in-person visit.

The pandemic taught me that a hug is so much more than putting your arms around someone. For some people, touch is like a superpower that gives them the energy they need to continue moving forward. Think about babies who lacked touch during crucial growing stages. Researchers have proven that babies not held, hugged, and coddled enough can stop growing. If the situation lasts long enough, they can even die. Now, do you see how important human connection is?

Grasping this information again, during a time when a lack of human connection was painfully too present, is precisely why I added CONNECT on the Ph.ME! Plan. I wanted a daily and weekly reminder to reach out to people who are either going through a tough time, are alone, might need inspiration to start over or start something new, or just to let someone I care about know I am thinking of them. This reminder also made me feel like my mission of having a full church at the end of my life, filled with people who knew they were important to me, would happen.

This card is also a reminder that I need to make every moment count and never waste a chance to tell someone how I feel. My friend Nikki, who I immediately bonded with when I moved to Wilmington, North Carolina, once said to me she learned when someone popped into her mind, it meant she needed to reach out. Hearing that made such an impression on me, I adopted that practice. I learned from observing how she nurtured her friendships.

On my Ph.ME! cards, on the CONNECT line, I write the name of a person I've been thinking of. I reach out to that person by phone, text, or email. Sometimes, I send a card or a small care package to make them smile or laugh. I often wonder if that gesture makes me equally as happy as the person to whom I sent the happiness.

In going back to my mission of a full church, I will say nothing would make me happier than to know all those people are reminiscing over the goofy things I said and did and are thankful for my help. If we are without great relationships at the end of our lives, what was it all for? And just having one or two strong relationships isn't enough for me. In the category of relationships, especially, I want it all.

I have been told throughout my life that I am a strong person, and I never really imagined that word when describing myself. But I now realize it absolutely describes who I am. That attribute is why many people talk to me about difficulties they are currently navigating that they know I have been through. After all, why not share with those we care about how we dealt with challenges, to save them from having to go through the same exact thing? To me, that feels like the best use of a crappy situation—to use it for someone else's benefit.

One of my absolute most dear friends, Tara, whom I have known since college, did just that. She sacrificed her comfort zone to have a difficult conversation with me to help me avoid a situation in which she knew I would wind up experiencing pain and devastation. She, of course, was right in her assessment, but the fact that we'd both taken time to nurture our friendship over the years is what made that conversation possible. It's people like her you will never forget and always cherish.

But nurturing relationships isn't only about the tough times. It's about celebrating the noteworthy moments in your life too. If you're on social media, think about those connections and how it makes you feel to know people are thinking of you enough to comment on your social post. There's a reason why social media is so addicting. Never mind the toxic parts that lead some people into a comparison trap; social media also has beneficial aspects. Those are when you connect with others you wouldn't be connecting with otherwise. Special moments when friends or social media contacts share personal stories and pictures of new babies, engagements, and reports on new homes and jobs, graduations, milestone birthdays, and anniversaries keep us unified to some degree.

Connection is also networking in the professional realm. Think about how much easier it is to get a job when you know someone who works where you would like to work. Have you ever pursued a career at a company without knowing anyone there? It was hard, wasn't it? It's always so much easier when someone internally can speak to your work ethic and skill set. Ultimately, the most essential part of connecting is to make it genuine. That's where the real magic happens.

Chapter Eleven

PROJECTS - LIFE IS SHORT, MAKE IT COUNT!

Create the life you can't wait to wake up to.
~ Evander Holyfield

If you're anything like me, you have several projects on your list. Fun projects—ones that make you anxious to pursue them. Now, I am not someone who enjoys sitting still, and I'm taking another guess about you: You don't either. I like to be busy and have multiple projects to juggle simultaneously. I enjoy learning new things, challenging myself, and meeting new people, so every time I take on a new project, I enjoy brainstorming with others, seeking advice from experts, and researching things I don't yet know about.

I look at it this way: Now that I am an adult and can do almost anything I want, the options are endless for fun things that I can delight in. Would I benefit from learning a new creative software program? Can I write a book and get it published? Do I want to redecorate my living room? Would taking photography, cooking, or creative writing classes be fun? Would I enjoy learning how to play pickleball? Should I create a new vision board to bring to light all the things I'd like in my life and serve as visual reminders?

Yes! Why not?

I have an entrepreneurial spirit. Typically, my projects involve exploring a product or a service idea I've dreamt up to see if it's been done. Whenever I have one of these *genius* ideas—a handful of times in my life—I get so excited to write things down about it. That way, I won't forget the exciting details which came to mind when the light bulb first went on. I imagine you've had those moments, too, the ones that immediately make you think to yourself: *I wonder if this idea would make life easier, more fun, or possibly help someone, or could it even become my career?!* You may also wonder: *Could this be my million-dollar idea?*

When these thoughts come into your mind, I strongly encourage you to write them down. One or all of them could very well be life-changing. When you notice yourself getting excited about the idea, that's precisely when you need to pull out your Ph.ME! Plan and get those thoughts on paper. Otherwise, that million-dollar idea may find itself on the back burner and get lost in outer space, along with all the other wasted discoveries and epiphanies. Don't let that happen. Make life count. Pursuing your ideas, dreams, and experiences that excite you is what makes your life so amazing.

What you write down on the Projects line of your Ph.ME! Plan can be anything that sparks your desire to get moving. It can be about turning your spare room into a home gym, ultimately leading you to exercise more, or it can be the book you want to write based on interviews of friends' horrible dating experiences and compile into one heck of a hilarious Dates From Hell memoir. Whatever it is, if it makes you happy, then it is likely a fantastic idea.

And who cares if it doesn't earn you a million dollars if you have fun doing it? If we stop learning and stop doing, we stop growing.

Now that you have this super-cool and compelling idea for your new project, I recommend you write it down weekly as a reminder to continue working on it. If you care enough to write it down, you care about the project. There is one project in particular I have written down for more than a decade. It means so much to me, and I believe in it so much. I have worked very hard on it here and there. But I haven't taken it to the finish line—yet. That is exactly why I continue to write it down. I know, when the time is right, I will finish it. Writing it down helps me not lose sight of the dream I will ultimately bring to fruition.

Your projects don't necessarily have to be something you do for yourself. They can be about helping a neighbor with her gardening or learning to speak sign language to communicate with a friend in your book club a little better to make her feel more involved. The point is it is an initiative, an effort, that is fulfilling, whether it benefits you or someone else.

The bottom line? Your project should tap into someplace truly meaningful that brings utter joy to your soul. I promise you, by following through on your projects, you will make your heart happy.

Chapter Twelve

PROJECTS - NEXT STEPS, MAKE THEM REAL!

*The ones who are crazy enough to think
they can change the world, are the ones who do.*
~ Steve Jobs

Now that you know the importance of projects, goals, and dreams, it's time to chase them down. Surely if you have a dream, you want to know a little about what it would take to get there.

Let's say that one of your goals is becoming a vice president at your company. Right now, you are in a manager role. Start by researching individuals who are currently VPs. Look at their LinkedIn profile or company bios online. What skills do they have that you don't?

There you go. Write those down on NEXT STEPS. Is there a mentoring program within your company or somewhere that's convenient for you? Join that club. If there isn't a mentoring program available, try finding an outline of one, present it to your boss, and request that you be a pilot member. That's a leadership skill of a VP if I've ever heard one.

What if one of your goals is a little trickier? What if you don't exactly know how to get started? Not to worry, because anything you want to know can be found on the internet, which will become your new best friend. Start here by entering related terms on a search engine and see what comes up. Go down some rabbit holes if you have to. Start reaching out to individuals and organizations and ask them for ten minutes of their time for an informational meeting. You may get ignored and hear a few nos. But, eventually, you'll get the answers you need, people to help you, or both.

Think about all the entrepreneurs in the world and when they started. Living in Atlanta, Georgia, I have often heard the story of how Sara Blakely created her iconic brand, the ridiculously successful Spanx. Her journey was not easy, not by any means. But she believed in her dreams and kept pursuing them. She didn't let it stop her when she was turned away and told that her product idea was silly and would never amount to anything. Why? Because it was *her* dream, not anyone else's. Now I know I have made that statement several times throughout the book. But that is because I want you to fully grasp the power behind a dream belonging to you and, in a way, being given to you. Sara Blakely believed in her heart her idea would be something special, which became her mission. Look where she is today. It's hard not to see Spanx products in every type of retail or online store these days. Even if you have to pursue your dream part-time, keep going.

Now, I'd like you to give this next question some considerable thought. How would you feel at the end of your life if you had a dream or goal that touched your heart so deeply, yet you never did anything about it? So what are you waiting for? You are still moving forward even if you do a few small things weekly.

One of the projects I would like to start is developing a creative way to frame old Broadway show Playbills and old baseball programs that belonged to my grandparents. My Nana was a huge fan of operas and musicals, and both my Nana and Poppi loved baseball. Showcasing things they had when they were younger would bring me a smile when I'd walk by them. I think it would make a fascinating piece of artwork.

My next steps in making this happen are to:

- Create a Pinterest board.

- Print out designs I like.

- Buy the materials needed.

- Set aside time for assembling.

An additional step to bringing your projects to life is to talk to your friends and family about your ideas. Studies show when you add in this element, the probability increases for the individual completing the project. I know the dream becomes much more real once I tell my friends and loved ones. And when I do, I speak of my projects with such excitement that those who know me best will continue asking me how they're coming along. I know this, so I also know it will be one of my motivators.

Most importantly, continue to write down your brilliant ideas. For me, writing my tasks and next steps down gives me an action-item list, making the project more manageable, and it motivates me to do what I want to do, eliminating the potential for putting it off or losing track. The great thing about this approach is it can apply to projects of any size.

Chapter Thirteen

WHAT IS YOUR WEEKLY HIGHLIGHT?

You're off to great places! Today is your day!
Your mountain is waiting so... get on your way!
~ Dr. Seuss

What if someone said they had a very unique gift *just for you?* That would feel pretty amazing. There's no doubt about that. Well, guess what? You get that special gift *every single day*. It's called that day.

What makes you smile? What things, people, situations, and activities make you genuinely happy, at peace, or feel you will have a phenomenal day? I'd like you to give this some real thought. Take a few minutes.

I'll tell you some of mine. The things on my list provide varying degrees and types of happiness. But let me assure you, every single thing on my list brings pure joy to my very existence.

My niece, Sidney, is one. This little human is the single, most important thing in my world. I can't even imagine having a child and feeling the love which goes along with that gift. I, however, have been blessed with a niece who, since she was one second old, has been my favorite person. She's smart, resourceful when she wants to be, kind, energetic, and she has had a sense of wit that rivals any *Saturday Night Live* comedian since she could talk. I have a million stories about her, but I will share just this one to express the type of happiness she brings to my life.

About eleven years ago, Sidney would have been five. I got a call just around 8:00 p.m. from her. I initially answered the phone expecting it to be my sister—because of caller ID, of course—but the first thing I heard after saying hello was, "Christi, pleeeease come to our house and help me make a leprechaun trap!"

Okay, so it was late, and I had work in the morning, with a forty-minute drive before I would even get to their house. "Okay," I said, "I'm on my way—let's make the best trap ever."

"Yay!" I heard.

That's all I need. I love that child beyond words, and quality time with her is always the highlight of my week. So, what, or who, in your life makes you feel that way? Do you make time for them as often as possible?

Take a moment to consider when you are happy. Imagine the feeling when you are smiling, laughing, totally involved in the task at hand; what do you see yourself doing? Who is with you? As I reflect on my life, I can come up with a list.

- Tennis. Oh yes, this game makes me feel like a kid. When I'm on a court, I'm in my happy place.

- Coke Slurpees on a hot day paired with a tennis match against my equally-as-competitive boyfriend, and that's, like, the pinnacle of afternoons.

- An evening alone and downtime with no have-to-do things on my list, starting with a long walk, listening to podcasts, and then coming home to make a frozen pizza while I watch a rom-com or horror movie. Anything with Kate Beckinsale or Ryan Reynolds, and I'm so in.

- Riding my mountain bike.

- Sitting in a beach chair around 5:00 p.m., watching the ocean and listening to the waves as the sun goes down.

- Live music—I have loved going to concerts since the very first one my mom took me to, which was the Styx Mr. Roboto tour. I was hooked right from the start.

- This next one truly is one of my favorite things in life: the laughter flows when I am together with my sister and my niece.

- Foot massages. There is a magical place near my home that has 70-minute foot massages for only $40. Talk about relaxing! You sit in a quiet room in a super comfy chair, the lights are dim, a fish tank is in the front, and you can hear a very faint whirring of the tank's motor, which is mesmerizing; there is soft music playing, and someone is rubbing your feet. It is heavenly.

That's my list. What do you think I would write down on my Ph.ME! card for my Weekly Highlight to bring some happiness to my week? Tennis and a Coke Slurpee, a long walk listening to a cool podcast, a foot massage, time with my niece? Yes, yes, yes!

I am lucky enough to have a job that I love. So, it's not like my days are filled with dread by any means. It's quite the opposite, actually, and I enjoy logging on to work. But you'd better believe, on this line of my Ph.ME! Plan, I'm writing down something that makes me feel like a kid or relaxed or excited. Why not? We are adults. For the most part, we create our own schedules. So, why wouldn't we make time for something that gives us an hour or two of pure happiness every week?

Now it's your turn. What makes your heart sing? When are you most relaxed, excited, happy? Create your list. Create your list and refer back to it often as a reminder of how you can make your life more meaningful.

There are so many days and weeks passing by when we don't put ourselves as a priority. That needs to change. It is imperative to incorporate time every day or week to do something *you* want to do for yourself. It's called self-love—trust me; it's vital for your well-being. A happier you allows you to be better to yourself and those around you.

Chapter Fourteen

HAVE YOU PLANNED YOUR NEXT ADVENTURE?

Find out who you are and do it on purpose.
~ Dolly Parton

First, I want to ask if you have ever been so terrified to do something, but you still wanted to do it. I imagine the answer is yes. We all have. I wanted to go ziplining, but I am terrified of heights. *Hmm. Okay, how is that going to work exactly?!* Sometimes, you must eliminate what scares you and roll with the rest.

An example of this is a trip I took one holiday season to the Dominican Republic with a friend and some of her friends. It was Christmas time, and this particular year I was celebrating a little differently than I normally did. From the beginning, her friends made it clear that complaining about every little thing at the magical luxury resort where we were staying was on their daily schedule. I had had enough, and my friend was in the same boat. Instead of sticking with the "Let's Be Miserable Club," she and I went to the front desk to see what excursion we could join to get the heck out of there for a day. Options included jeep riding, snorkeling, and ziplining. The obvious choice was ziplining because it made my heart race with a twinge of: *I've always heard it's so much fun.* Sold!

Here we go on what turned out to be a wild, unexpected adventure, one I will always remember for the tremendous meaning it holds. The drive through town, headed toward the mountain, was one of my favorite Christmas gifts that year. I was blessed by seeing dozens of smiles on the faces of beautiful, happy local children, waving boldly to us as we drove by, seemingly just because we were something they had never seen before. On the ride up the mountain, I spoke to God the entire way. Part of that internal conversation was me negotiating with Him like I have done many times before. It went something like, "Okay, God. I am having a miserable time, and it is Christmas! PLEASE remove my fear the second I step out of this jeep and let me enjoy this adventure I am about to go on. I need this so badly, and all I want is to enjoy my vacation."

I would say what I share next miraculously happened, but we all know exactly who made it happen. The moment I walked up to the first run, 0 percent of me was afraid, and this feeling lasted throughout the entire ziplining trip—as in *zero*. I found myself standing on ledges overlooking treetops, feeling very sure-footed, without a single quiver in my knees. That had never happened in my entire life.

I am usually the person who gets slightly shaky when I am standing on a high balcony behind a guardrail. That day in the Dominican Republic, I felt myself smiling like never before, as I was able to look at my surroundings from high above and through such a different lens. I zip-lined down each run with my eyes open wider than ever, with shrieks of pure joy and a heart full of such gratefulness that God heard my prayer and delivered in the biggest way ever.

That adventure was about eight years ago, and I haven't had one like it since. This very thought leads me to my next story—the story of when I met my friend Katrina—the quintessential adventure seeker.

My friend Britt and I went to church to join a small group, which felt like being at a bar where we were supposed to pick up new friends and form a group based on one short dialogue. I seriously did not enjoy it at first. In one conversation, a woman adamantly responded to my question about where the groups met, that they did not meet at restaurants because it was not about drinking; it was about Jesus. Point taken, sister. The point in question was she and I would not be in a group together. In my world, Jesus enjoyed a good glass of wine now and then. So, Britt and I kept looking for our people.

We eventually spotted Katrina, and she looked like us. *Us* being youngish, fun, and as if she'd want to get closer to God every Monday evening and occasionally enjoy a cocktail during those meetings if the need arose. Which it often did. But, hey, I grew up Catholic, and my people enjoy wine. So, as far as I am concerned, wine is A-OK for church-related gatherings. We all became a tight-knit group, and many of us have become best friends. Katrina is one of them.

Katrina knows the true meaning of adventure. I often wish that I was adventurous like she is, and I tell her this every time she talks about a new mission trip she is going on or a fun adventure she has planned.

Her latest one was an African safari. She and I had talked about doing this together, but I could not commit to doing it right away because of where my life was with trying to get back on track. It was easy to see that her passion for going on this trip was intense, so the night she told me she had booked the trip made me so happy. Even though I could not go, I was elated to hear she was off on another adventure.

Katrina's vivacious spirit for seeing the world is something I have always admired, and I admire even more her willingness to explore alone to fulfill her dreams. Now, that is brave and undoubtedly adds to the level of exhilaration to be in charge of everything because there is no one else there to do things for her. I always ask her if she is afraid or nervous about traveling by herself, and every time her answer is the same: nope. The fact she is getting out there, exploring the world, and experiencing things that make her feel so alive is incredibly motivating. It impresses me because so many people talk about the adventurous things they want to do, but very few actually do them.

Thinking about my friend's eagerness for discovery makes me wonder how I will feel when I am old and unable to travel. Will I be able to say I saw the world and had as many exciting experiences as I would have planned for had I mapped out my life and paid more attention to adventure over the menial day-to-day stuff that does not enrich my life a bit? Will I have done enough? Will I have seen enough and met enough people to equate to the life I wish for myself right now while I am still young enough to do these things?

When those thoughts pop into my head, it makes me realize even more that my friend is living out the adventure part of her life exactly how it should be done, with no regrets. She inspires me to continue seeking adventure, even if it is close to home. It is not the destination that matters; it is how much it makes you smile, takes your breath away, and makes you feel alive. Knowing Katrina makes me strive to regularly look at things through a new lens in hopes of discovering something miraculous, beautiful, or different in my everyday surroundings. Even if it is a tiny adventure I can grab hold of in my daily life, I will take it.

You are never too old to seek and enjoy the unknown, situations that get your heart racing. Go ahead, be an explorer of life— whatever that means to you in whatever stage of your life. Just make sure the *adventure* makes you feel like you have checked something significant off your bucket list, allows you to revel in something entirely new, and makes you feel like you are living life to the fullest. If it ignites a spark, then you are on the right track.

At the end of my life, I want to be able to answer yes to this question. Actually, I want to be able to respond with a "Hell *yeah*, I did!"

Have I experienced enough in my life?

Have you?

Chapter Fifteen

I AM GRATEFUL FOR . . .

Delayed answers to prayers can often be the evidence that God is doing something BIGGER you didn't even think of.
~ Unknown

In life, there are so many ups and downs. It's so much easier to be grateful for the wonderful things that make us feel we are living in abundance. Things like landing the perfect job and earning far more than you ever imagined; meeting your soulmate who is the ideal combination of fun, intelligent, successful, and attractive; or snagging your dream home at a phenomenal price.

But what about those times when you are not the cherry on top of the sundae? The days, weeks, or months when life is just routine and not delivering anything grandiose? Maybe you have a job but can't see yourself doing it for the rest of your life. You may own a home, but it may not be your dream home. And, maybe, life is just average right now, with no ups or downs.

I have learned I can be grateful for things that happen which aren't necessarily considered *good* by traditional standards. Or, at least, they don't start that way. I can also be thankful for the quiet times when nothing good or bad is happening: when life just is. I think we can all recall a time or two in life when something frustrating or heartbreaking occurred, and then, miraculously, the situation opened us up to something that wouldn't have happened otherwise. Sometimes people call those unanswered prayers, or they say when one door closes, another door opens. There are lots of sayings that encompass this. And I believe them. I've had several unanswered prayers myself. Since I genuinely feel God created us to be happy, I am thankful for many of those prayers going unheard.

Now, think about the things you are grateful for that didn't start as something good. What happened that made you grateful for the situation? Did you also learn from it? Odds are you did. That is also something to be thankful for. If we view life as one big series of events we can learn from and benefit from magnificently, I think more of us would be living a life filled with contentment and optimism.

I've had job interviews in which I am asked to describe a difficult situation and then explain how I managed it. I find it amusing that I often explain those situations as ones for which I am so thankful. *I am thankful I had a boss who had anger issues and took them out on me.* Yeah, I know that's crazy. And, trust me, it sucked at the time. But I'm grateful it made me stronger and more resilient in business. It helped me become better at focusing on the tasks and leaving out the emotions.

People who know me well probably wouldn't describe me as someone with a thick skin. But because of several situations in my life, I have developed one. Friends and family often come to me when they are living through a difficult time. They know

I can set aside emotion from what is happening and help them calmly figure out what's going on, set a plan, and help move them forward. I can leave out any prejudice toward any party while looking at the situation as a transaction to help my friend or family member get through it as swiftly and as pain-free as possible.

When God gives you a new beginning, it starts with an ending.
Be thankful for closed doors. They often guide us to the right one.
~ Unknown

So, I encourage you to dig deep on this one and write down what you are grateful for that has profoundly impacted your life.

Chapter Sixteen

I AM EXCITED ABOUT . . .

Your life should be a story you are excited to tell.
~ Adam Braun

What are you excited about this week? My initial thought is if you don't have anything to write on this line, that is no bueno. There must be something you have to be excited about this week. It can be small; for instance, I am excited about getting off work a few hours early on Friday.

Here are some other theoretical examples:

- *I am excited to play tennis with my team and go for margaritas afterward.*

- *I am excited to start my fulfilling, rewarding new job.* It doesn't matter if you have a new job; but if you want one, I suggest you write it on the "I am excited about" line of your Ph.ME! card.

Have you heard about manifesting? It works. It's easy, it's free, and it's rewarding because it is life-changing.

So now, let's try this again. What are you excited about? Trying something new that puts you out of your comfort zone, testing your new self-challenge of being more assertive, your soulmate who is coming into your life soon, the baby God is bringing you, the fitness program you've started and that makes you happy to join a new gym?

What I am excited about is this book and the product I created to go along with it. I wholeheartedly believe in the Ph.ME! cards. For years, I have been writing down what I want in my life, what I am thankful for, and what I am excited about. I just never realized it was a proven process and an actual thing everyone should be doing to enjoy a happier, more fulfilled life.

But look at me now—it *is* a thing. Something that has always helped me be, feel, and do better is now helping others. I could not be happier. I am excited about changing lives, which is the whole point of this book and product.

By committing to writing down all the things we have discussed on your Ph.ME! cards every week, by making it a habit, you are essentially making your list of the things that will enrich your life. And you are making it the type of life that makes you jump out of bed every day because you are eager to live it. You are also making a visual cue for yourself, which helps increase exponentially the probability of these things coming into being. I strongly encourage you to not only write about things that have already happened, or you know will happen, but also about the ones you *want* to happen. Preparing for how amazing that next chapter will be will only help solidify its entrance into your life.

I am excited about next summer's vacation in Seaside, where my future beach house is. My vacation will give me a perfect chance to search for exactly where I'd like my oceanfront property to be. Coincidentally, I was in Seaside with my sister and my niece a few summers ago. We were having dinner at a restaurant overlooking the beach one night, and I pointed to a beautiful grassy area with white Adirondack chairs where the rays of the sunset were hitting it so perfectly it looked romantic and magical.

I turned to my sister and said, "That will make an excellent spot for my wedding and reception, don't you think?" She smiled and half-laughed because she knew it would come true once I said it and put it out there. I am super excited about that coming to fruition.

Let's figure out where your passions lie and what will make your heart happy. Are you not in a job you love? Could you be excited about your next rewarding and fulfilling career? There are a handful of spots on your Ph.ME! cards where you can jot down things relating to that. Are you excited to heal from a difficult situation you have been through, or perhaps looking forward to brainstorming with a friend who also wants to launch a custom T-shirt line like you do? Whatever you are excited about, own it.

Once you own it, write down supportive tools, practices, and circumstances that will help you accomplish it. Write down your ideas and the thoughts that allow you to see those things happening. Look at those reminders daily and repeat the process until your goal is achieved.

Chapter Seventeen

I AM

Dear Self,
I AM going to make you so proud.

~ Unknown

I AM!

Discovering and boldly professing who and what you are is a powerful behavior to implement into your life. For this, I'd like you to write who and what you think you are. By this, I do not mean that you are an Asian-American woman or a thirty-five-year-old businesswoman. But, really, *who* are you? Or, better yet, who would you like to be and how would you like to see yourself?

Let me give some examples to help narrow down what may speak to you:

- *I AM brave.*

- *I AM inspirational.*

- *I AM creative and resourceful.*

- *I AM healthy and have a positive outlook on life.*

- *I AM worthy of love.*

- *I AM thriving.*

- *I AM excellent at building successful businesses.*

I think you get the idea. Now, I would like you to take this one step further. Write down things you would like to come to fruition, whether they are true or not, with the mindset they are definitely going to happen:

- *I AM having a baby.*

- *I AM promoted to VP of Sales.*

- *I AM purchasing my dream home.*

- *I AM so in love with my spouse.*

- *I AM achieving financial stability.*

- *I AM appreciating everything that is going my way.*

- *I AM attending Wake Forest University.*

There's a great deal of science describing the connection between consistently writing your desire and successfully practicing the activity being linked with having it come true. It creates a habit and changes your mindset. Eventually, these aspirations will become your reality.

What would you like that you can write down as an "in the present" statement?

What about:

- *I am healthy and feeling stronger than I have in a long time.*

- *I am thankful I have enough money to buy my dream home.*

- *I am loving my job as the new director of marketing.*

I wrote a similar statement daily during my seven-month stint of unemployment during the pandemic. I mean, really—*I love my job*—when I didn't even have one!? Yes, I seriously wrote that down, even while I was partially consumed with the possibility of having to move because I was draining my savings. I knew I wasn't alone in my worry, but that thought didn't make me feel any better.

If you are wondering: *Wasn't that difficult to do when you were jobless?* Yes. But, writing that down as if it were actually happening in the present gave me hope and eventually made me feel confident I deserved it and my dream job would surface when the timing was right. Putting down that positive affirmation with a pen to paper over and over gave me a sense of peace. It allowed me to maintain focus and keep moving forward. It allowed me to continue being positive and enjoy the good things in my life rather than wish for time to speed by. All along, I believed deep down, a great opportunity would present itself. Writing I was happy about my new job when I didn't even have one yet was an essential declaration that helped get me the fantastic job I knew was waiting for me.

When I initially wrote my statement for I AM, I was not I AM-ing big enough. I had written down that I was happy in my new job. That's good and all, but it wasn't big enough. So I wound up getting a job that made me happy. I learned new skills, met friendly new people, and felt I was in a place where I could grow. But a few months down the road, while the pandemic was still plaguing the economy, the company ended my contract because they were down in revenue. I won't lie; I was distraught for a solid twenty-four hours. But I always try to sleep on things and see how I feel in the morning. I woke up the next day feeling the job I had written down wasn't the one I really wanted and knew I deserved.

At the time, I was working on a side business and trying to build that up. I made money on small projects, but it wasn't my dream situation. I got back on track and wrote in my notebook every day that what I was doing was leading me to my dream job, and I reminded myself I was lucky to have it. Because of this, I started to embrace what I was doing, giving myself a purpose. It also took away feelings of being in limbo.

After receiving several rejections for jobs I had interviewed for, ones that seemed fine but I wasn't overjoyed about, I finally got a call from a recruiter on *the one*. The old saying, *you know when you know*, hit me when I met the people who are now my work family. Feeling comfortable within the work family is high on my list of must-haves when considering whether to take a job.

Not only did I obtain a job I love that is rewarding and challenging and provides an abundance of growth and learning opportunities, but also the job is one with a dream commute, and I am so proud to tell people who I work for. I now have a job that doesn't always feel like work because I can honestly say I love what I do.

You can have this too.

Another thing I often write down after I AM is that I am thrilled to have the best husband in the world. The backstory here is that I am not married. And I often haven't had a boyfriend when I've written that down. However, I now have a pretty fantastic boyfriend who I feel lucky to have in my life. Regularly writing this down allowed me to smile when I envisioned this person and what he did to improve my life. The boyfriend now is not a husband, but, trust me, he has improved my life. I'm telling you, this works.

I want you to go big. Dream the biggest dream you can think of and put pen to paper.

Now switching to a different tone, I want to address speaking your I AM on a much more serious note. This pertains to a close friend, the life of any gathering, and a serious walking ray of sunshine—my dear friend Kerry. I have always loved her spirit, and it immediately drew me to her in the first place and allowed us to become the best of friends. Before our lives took us in different directions, knowing I would see her often when we lived in the same city always made that day the best. Not long ago, Kerry told me her cancer had returned and that it was terminal. In true Kerry fashion, after telling me her cancer was terminal, she said, "I AM going to beat it, though, because I AM a fighter." And she is.

Now switching gears again, to a time in my life when I was considering where to attend college. I had visited a friend at the college she went to and decided from the moment I stepped on the campus that it felt like home and I would be attending the following fall. When I returned home and told my mom, she quickly replied, "People like us don't go to a university like that." What she meant was there was no way she could afford it. She was a single mom who worked her butt off to provide for us. Through no fault of her own, she wasn't dreaming big enough. That was okay because I was dreaming big enough for myself. Maybe it was the challenge I needed—for someone to tell me it wasn't meant for me. But as I have mentioned, my dream is my dream and doesn't belong to someone else. Long story short: I am sure you can guess where I attended college that next fall.

And so, I religiously wrote down in my journal "Stetson University" because I knew I would eventually be a student there. I looked at that note daily and created action items in my mind and on paper to help make my dream come true.

Once I got there, I met a great friend, Jyl, and she and I wrote down things we wanted to happen all the time—mostly in social situations. We did this to give ourselves confidence, but we had no idea that writing down our game plan truly was more powerful than we ever imagined. All we knew was that it worked. So we kept on doing it.

Years later, I began writing down things I wanted for myself, and I would put that piece of paper in the side pocket of my car. I would look at it all the time and eventually started crossing off the things on my list I had accomplished. I used this powerful approach having no idea of the science behind it, and I realized I should be doing this all the time.

Many people have been through challenging circumstances, especially in the last few years. Friends and relatives have and are currently dealing with complicated situations—such as the loss of a parent, a spouse leaving, job security, issues with pregnancy, lingering health concerns—and wondering where they are in life or whether their career is where it should be. None of these are concerns that can easily be solved by writing down I AM (fill in the blank). But it is a start. Whatever your issue is, whatever you need to claim as your own, I AM it. If you are reading this book, you can absolutely say: *I AM a strong, hopeful, resourceful person.*

You can write anything you want to. It's your pen, your thought, and your vision.

I will leave you with one final thought. I AM going to work with Jack Canfield, Rhonda Byrne, and Dr. John Demartini on my book and the Ph.ME! Plan. This has been something I have proclaimed all along. I have written this aspiration down many times and have verbalized it just as many times. I AM confident that it will happen.

I AM also confident that *you* will experience a better, more fulfilled life by implementing these things into your life.

The biggest adventure you can ever take
is to live the life of your dreams.
~ Oprah Winfrey

Chapter Eighteen

I WILL

Obstacles don't have to stop you. If you run into a wall,
don't turn around and give up. Figure out how to climb it.
Go through it or work around it.

~ Michael Jordan

It all comes down to this. The I WILL is where everything
you've been writing down, planning, and envisioning becomes
a reality. Why? Because the very concept of saying I WILL is
about taking action and believing in something so much that
you are making a definitive statement to let the world, and
more importantly YOU, know that you mean business.

I WILL is more significant than being hopeful or excited.
It's like an add-on to I Am. Declaring I WILL is a powerful
affirmation that goes beyond mere words—it is a commitment
and a proclamation of intent. By vocalizing these two simple
words, you are consciously deciding to take control of your
destiny and shape your own narrative. This declaration signifies
a shift from passive contemplation to active engagement,
propelling you toward a future you actively desire and design.

The significance lies in the transformative nature of this
statement. I WILL embodies determination, resolve, and a

willingness to embrace the challenges of pursuing what is truly important to you. It marks the beginning of a journey where you translate your aspirations into concrete actions, setting the stage for personal and professional accomplishments.

This declaration is about taking responsibility for your dreams and aspirations. It's a commitment to put in the effort, time, and energy required to turn your goals into reality. By saying I WILL, you give power to the agency you have in steering your life in the direction you choose.

The best part is that this proactive mindset will likely contribute to a more fulfilling life. It fosters a sense of purpose, accomplishment, and self-empowerment. Instead of being a passive observer, you become an active participant in your own story--earning the ultimate degree in YOU. The I WILL attitude is a catalyst for personal growth, resilience, and adaptability—crucial for navigating life's twists and turns. It is about taking intentional steps toward what truly matters to you. It is a commitment to continuous improvement and a recognition that you are the master of your own life.

As the final step in this journey to creating an ultimate awareness of what gives us purpose and provides a life of joy and discovery, what will you declare your I WILL statement to be? Just remember, as you put pen to paper. . .

> *Dare to dream, then decide to do.*
> ~Annette White

Next Steps

To download a free copy of the Ph.ME! cards referenced throughout the book, please visit

www.phmeplan.com and enter code:
MASTERLIFETODAY on the contact page.

To work with Christi, please contact:
cbaconsultingsolutions@gmail.com.

About the Author

Christi Burton is a marketing expert with twenty years of experience in marketing, project management, sales, branding, and growth strategy for large-scale, powerhouse organizations, such as the Turner Networks and Vera Bradley, as well as small, independently owned companies. Christi is also an active copywriter with more than 150 published articles and press releases written for well-known individuals, including *The Secret's* Rhonda Byrne; *Chicken Soup for the Soul* book series co-author Jack Canfield; and legendary thought leader and author Bob Proctor.

Christi developed a unique gift product that received multiple awards, including Best New Product at the National Stationery Show in NYC in 2008. That same product attracted the attention of ABC's *Shark Tank*.

The start of Christi's entrepreneurial journey began in NYC, where she was born. Her love of the beach came shortly after, as she was raised in Naples, Florida. Christi received a Bachelor of Arts degree from Stetson University. She currently lives in Atlanta, Georgia. Written on her Ph.ME! Plan is to ultimately retire at her amazing beach house someday.